British Library Cataloguing in Publication Data
A catalogue record for this book is available from the British Library.
ISBN 978-0-9560303-5-1

Design, Layout & Typesetting by be...creative
Home Farm Office, Eamont Bridge, Penrith, Cumbria CA10 2BX
www.becreativecumbria.co.uk

Cover picture: Iona cross of driftwood and rope- Camas, Isle of Mull

Yours, Faithfully

Stephen G Wright

Introduction

The Christian cross is rich with symbolism. I draw on that symbolism here, most especially the cross that has come to be associated with Iona, the cross with a circle. The horizontal beam can be seen as symbolic of the transcendent, transpersonal, unknowable God; indefinable, beyond words, reaching out boundlessly inside and outside of space and time. The vertical beam is the direct line of communication from above to below, the immanent God, personal, knowable; the one in and with whom we can have a relationship, closer to us than our own breath, knowing us better then we know ourselves. The circle binds and holds both in harmony; and at the centre is the point of intersection where all duality is lost and all possibility is contained.

All possibility - of a relationship in the Beloved that is outwith the realm of words and concepts; simultaneously deeply intimate. In these poems I seek to express some of that intimacy, the dance with the Beloved, the Friend, with whom we can chat as freely as the person in the next seat and find words bubbling up out of feelings and images. The One who teases and tempts; the trickster who plays with words and feelings to draw us deeper into relationship, into knowing. A boundless journey of infinite possibility, for if the soul is of God, and God is infinite, then the soul is infinite too. The dance between the two, where two become One, separating and joining, is the very dance of life itself.

Those, like me, who have followed the Contemplative Way, or have simply sat and heard the promptings of that still, small voice, have often sought to capture some hint of what it is like to hear and feel that inner connection. An interior experience that, with due discernment, is not just a personal, blissful high, but a transformative influence that takes us out of spiritual navel gazing and changes the way we are in the world; the movement within fosters movement without, seeking to take the illuminations, the inner strengthening of the God-I relationship, the piercing insights of truth to be of service in the world in some way. Inward listening is not a passive dropping out from the world, but an active turning inwards only to turn outwards into worldly commitment to service.

The verses in these pages arise from that inner prompting. Here, in two parts, are representations of that internal dialogue, where me talks to and listens to You, soul to Source, person to Divine... imaginings, feelings, impressions, memories flushing words to the surface to try to capture the essence of the relationship, the dance between two that is One. Words always fail, fall short, but they can come close. It is easy to know one, it is easy to know two, but to know that one and one are two we have to understand the *and*.

Poems are ways of knowing the *and*. Poetry opens us to ways of comprehending the Divine because it touches both out thoughts and feelings. Although the poetry here is expressed as dialogue between the soul and God, the reality is far more subtle – an exuberant interplay in relationship as with any relationship, sometimes joyous sometimes challenging, sometimes serious sometimes jocular, sometimes direct sometimes elliptical…. And as with all relationships, getting to know each other in ways where words can only skirt around the edges of what we come to feel and know about the other, about Love.

In this relationship there is momentarily two as personal identity stands apart from God, knowing the pain of separation, but also the joy of being separate which permits the seeing and knowing of God and All-That-Is, permits relating as two, permits the potential of re-union. Words slip and slide as I try to explain this, perhaps it is no wonder that the mystically inclined have found it hard to be accepted in some religions where hard facts and God as a separate, forbidding 'other' is what counts.

So here, me with a small 'm' and 'you' with a small 'y' always refers to the personal soul, You and Me when capitalised is always the Divine. Thus there is distinction, separateness which permits dialogue; an element of the constant dance between duality and oneness, separate identity and union. Is that a revelation, at least in part and without getting into complex theology, of the profound paradox of 'I and the Father are One' (John 10:30)? For two to know One there must be two.

Thus these poems are a dialogue between the lover and the Beloved, between soul and its Source. All, in the end, are conversations in and about Love. They fall into several groups.

Sometimes they are grounded in time as a memory is flushed to the surface and, with the benefit of ageing and perhaps a little maturation, seen in a new light. When I was a child I couldn't understand what all the talk about God as something somewhere else was all about, I just knew that there was no separation, "Summer days" seeks to express something of that. "Important" looks at the impact of shedding our ego agendas as we get older, which also is a spiritual practice of letting go of our egocentrism as in "Periphysion" and the affectionate reflection of lurching from childhood to the present when we visit a place full of memories. The epiphany of getting old ("Nightmare of Gerontius") is contrasted but finds common ground in childhood reflections ("Whitsuntide", "Yellow Blanket") as the child seeks to know God and the comfort of a blanket mirrors an understanding of God that comes with mature years. "KJB", on the other hand, written in the year of the anniversary of the King James Bible, shows how in order to get to know God we have to unlearn some early less that positive lessons about God. "Red Admiral" (my favourite butterfly) draws on a childhood moment ingrained in my memory, and how butterflies, symbols of transformation, can have new import for us later in life.

Sometimes a seemingly random incident can spark a sudden awareness of the Presence and a reflection of the nature of that relationship. An experience in a "Waiting Room" dwells the nature of a life as a kind of waiting room for what comes after whilst "The Library" hints at the book-like creation of our own lives. In "Lookalikes" I muse upon how couples in close relationship tend to look like each other (so what happens when we form a relationship in God?). With "The Egg" the use of an unusual word by a seven-year-old grandchild prompts an inner dialogue in the midst of an ordinary domestic scene and also a short discourse on 'reality'. T S Eliot famously wrote that we cannot bear very much reality, but that depends on our understanding of reality. The 'real reality', the God to which the mystics refer, now that is another thing altogether of which we can never get enough. "The Disease" and "Spaces" explore the possibility of the God delusion, especially when we experience a crisis in life and "Summer Storm" reflects on how we create dualities with experiences that we judge good or bad. "Industrial Relations" is a meditation occurring in the midst of a TV debate about union rights, which prompted an inner dialogue about what "rights" we might have if we "work" for God! "Lent" and "Field of Dreams" likewise are prompted by seasonal experiences and the realisation of the light in all.

In part 2, the dialogue, at least the imagined dialogue, is reversed. The wings of the imagination carry the mystical experience, looking for words to express a feeling, a knowing, such as I explored in a longer poem elsewhere *("Beloved", SSP, 2012)*. Are they true? The spiritual practice of discernment summons us in Paul's words to "Test everything" (1 Thess. 5:21) for the boundary between mysticism and madness is wafer thin.

Some of the poems in this group touch on the immediacy and nature of God's Presence no matter where we are, what judgements about 'good' or 'bad' we make or how difficult we think it might be to connect ("Jump", "Lonesome Pine", "Prayer in Heaven", "The Rose", "Eternity", "Gorbalsiona"). Others subvert the 'programming' that many of us endured in childhood about the nature of God and Christ as remote and forbidding ("Dry Land", "Invitation", "The Claxon", "The Salesman", "Cairns"). In some we find hope in doubt and adversity ("The Missed Boat", "Faith", "On The Stage", "Crows", "Promise", "Terminal", "The Direction") or encouragement to give time for the relationship with God to develop and the soul to flourish ("Savouring", "Findhorn Bay", "The Gaze", "Great Expectation").

Others offer encouragement to let go of our ego agendas, embrace our history and go beyond it to ponder the liberation of the soul, ultimately invited to savour God beyond words ("Confession", "Commandment", "Since You Asked", "Silence", "Auto da Fe").

All these words are about intimacy of relationship. They assume that for each of us it is possible to have that deep spiritual inner conversation which words struggle to represent. That possibility is not universally anticipated or even approved of in some of our religions, yet it is the realm of the faith-full and the faith-empty down the ages, the possibility of intimate communion, as offered by the Master, Jesus, himself. And like the Master, the response beyond the surface words whether fierce, teasing, playful or humorous – is always encouraging and loving.

Like slow food, please see these poems as slow words. To be read and savoured for layers of meaning, a source of reflection upon your relationship in and with the Divine, meditations on love through the offering, presence and experience of Divine Love.

Stephen Wright
January 2014

Part 1

me to You

Summer days

I remember fields like this, when I was a child.
Fields like this. And walking with uncle Bob when he
said "This is a daisy" and "This is a buttercup" and
"This is a meadow brown." And I thought "How
strange, his knowledge of the details."
Because all I could see was You.

I remember a beach like this, empty of people and
no sound but the waves and a sudden feeling of
being entirely alone in the whole world and held
in place only by the embrace of cliffs remote to north
and south. Then my dad coming up behind me in the
dunes saying, "You can smell the sea. It's grand.
Smell that sea." And all I could smell was You.

I remember a sky like this, blue in blue, and lying
back in the long grass so the world disappeared,
reduced to a circumference of overhanging stems
and seed heads, unmoved on a windless day. And
Dyson, like me an escapee from school, lying out of
view and calling, "Listen to the bees zooming, and
way up there you can see him, hear him, singing his
heart out, a skylark." And all I could hear was You.

The particular sensory receptors engaged are of no consequence.
Description or differentiation is only a matter of interpretation,
influenced by custom and practice and the long slow formation
from nappy to shroud. Detailed dissections and discriminations
are useful for analytical understanding, even survival,
or at least the right way to pay the electricity bill or
get to the train on time. After that, I mean way after that,
they are liquefied, without purpose. Except
(and no minor exception) to reflect You, back, to You.

Lookalikes

How we become like each other.
Dog and dogged walk the same way,
bear the same expressions.
After 40 years of marriage Harry
and Sylvia look alike 'though he denies
the earrings. And Peter and Michael
wave to their arriving friend by the
airport "NO ENTRY" in ignorance of
their hands, chopping the air in
identical rhythm. If I hang around
with You, how long would it take?
How many conversations, how
many encounters, how many
prayers before someone says
"You look just like Him!" or "He
looks just like You!" If I apply this
theory with a lifetime of discipline and
gradual surrender, will I look at You
and see me? Will You look at me
and see You?

The egg

The egg was indeterminate.
He was only seven,
but he said "indeterminate".
Not hard or
soft boiled, neither one nor the other.
It set him up for the day,
a kind of melancholy,
of expectation that something
would go wrong. I think he was learning
that something could go wrong.

Hope slipped into the septic tank of relationships.
Fermented. Oozed. Bringing fertility to words
to passions. Not yet desiccated by exposure
to the fierce winds of reality.

We can never get enough reality. The poet
was wrong. My soul is insatiable for You. Thirst
bifurcates self-replicating longing. The I that is
not I rejects such desperation, seeking comfort
in safe boundaries, the predictably unpredictable,
the patterns and routines that corral the possibility
of randomly escaping perceptions.

I heard You.
"How are you managing?
How are you coping?
Are you free or subject to some device?"
Like his egg my life has become
Indeterminate.
OK.
Over to You.

Important

It seemed important at the time.
It all seemed important at the time.
All those appointments, that big diary.
All those pieces of work. Important.
Those goals. Achievements.

Nothing changed. Oh at least not
underneath. The pattern appeared
different, new, in the glinting sunlight
of the present moment. But,
and it's a big but, underneath
nothing was different.

What took place on the surface was superficial,
cosmetic. Under the surface impression
of the children's faces , the smiles
in the restaurant, under the
assumptions of differentness
there's a deep radiating something.
Something to do with You.

I can't quite put my finger on it
and the more I think about it
the more it slips away. But I'm quite
sure that underneath, it all just stays
the same. Not like history repeating
itself, no, not like that. It's more
there's really no history. Just
underneath, a stillness, a perpetuity.

Yellow blanket

The kind of summer day when the clouds come,
big clouds,
the kind of big clouds that stretch themselves
to occupy the whole sky,
claiming ownership as if the blue had no rights of her own.
They pass over or rather beneath the blue having nowhere to go,
no mission to complete.

When the clouds have their way
the shadows evaporate
and a cold wind sneaks in
exposing the inadvisability of my shorts.
But being bored and restless, the clouds
move on and the sun returns the heat
from the forgiving boundless blue.

I was in the back garden wrapped in bliss,
flat out on the dry lawn,
rolled in the yellow blanket my mum took off my bed.
"You'd better pick off the bits of grass, 'cause I'm not"
said the back of my mum in her pinny
going through the blue back door.
(Council house blue).

"All right" I said to the closed door.
I was in union in the warm blanket and
the cold breeze had no power over me.
Enmeshed in delight, cosy within cold.
Like I was being held by You.

Now I am an old man
sitting on my history
and listening to the last of the summer birds.
They've gone much quieter.
Not much left to shout about now.
The late summer has cleared
the rented accommodation and autumn
is queuing to take over the tenancy.

This new blanket is like summer, snug,
still warm with cool autumn outside it.
A blanket, a breeze and the end of summer sun.
Everything is moving on, but I can't help feeling that
I'm still being held, whether I'm six or sixty.
I always have been really, it's just that sometimes
I forgot.
It doesn't matter now.

Wrapping myself in a warm blanket
on a cold day I got to know what it feels like,
what You feel like.
It's one of the ways You like us to get to know You isn't it?
We can choose the colour, You have plenty.
And the time.
You have all the time in the world.
Just allowing ourselves to be wrapped in a warm woollen blanket.
Forever.

The disease

The disease is frightening and the river lay before me.
The ford eluded me.
I stuck with the bank, but on my right hand I could hear You daring me.
The church and cross, over the river, silent and indifferent under a midday sun.
A buzzard crossed before me, the shadow of her wing touched my forehead.

Is this the shallowed point?
The sand and mud less quick, less hungry?
Boots and trousers off, deep breath, go for it.
My wet boxers were the only ones to complain when my feet squeezed through the mud to the opposite bank.
Fierce river water up to my neck, my possessions held higher.
In exhilaration I learned: a response to a frightening disease is to do something more frightening.

On the bank.
No one about.
I left the boots and jeans off, feeling the good earth beneath my feet and the welcome air about my thighs.
I'm not sure.
Did I walk to the church or did it come to me?

St. John was nowhere to be seen (though the notice proclaimed his ownership).
In the cool of his house there You were, solemn in stained glass staring back at me.
The salt water, my eyes and the estuary, were in harmony.

Such an impossible demand, to plunge into such bereavement.
If not You, then who?
Was this an invitation, to cross the river, there to find a different view?
Or a casting off into the downdraft of annihilation;
nothingness and emptiness in holy matrimony birthing only despair.

Are You there across that water, in some other form, some other union?
Or will I discover You are just a trick of the mind invented to comfort me against the bitterness of aching reality wherein there is no other reality?

Wait.

To leave this church or stay.
I hesitated by the door and collapsed into pew number 3.
Head in hand.
Close and closed to tears.
A scream stuck somewhere in the middle.
I saw something.
An irrevocable blackness.
The fruits of meaninglessness of life, my life, all life.
Just happening without reason or rhyme.
No purpose, no other, no transcendent possibility,
An abyss without hope, expectation or possibility of You.

Is this what we rail against?
Lurking at the heart of every human
or dream judged good or bad;
an essential heartlessness?
You, a trick of the mind invented to keep the abyss at bay.
Every human endeavour invented to keep the abyss at bay.
Absolute mortality.
Absolute nothingness.
Futility.

Can I live with this, or die with this, without You?
Is this clinging to You just Canute keeping back the tide of fear?

Is the truth of Your absence the truth that lies at the heart of all men and women?
Is that the truth, that there is no hope even of doubt, the only certainty nothing?

Can it be the truth; that You want me to walk away from You
to find a new relationship?
Or is there no You to want such a relationship at all.
Is it all fearful fabrication to keep the fear of fabrication at bay?
Even fear of nothing is someday pulled into nothing;
Not even the fear of fear is left.

I left without saying goodbye, just to try it out.
The pain was not too great.
I stood before the old cross and tried to pray
and thought of TS and waiting without hope.
Suppose I try it without You? Without them?
It's a pain like I have not had before. Is this agony?
Still, I looked around the churchyard and followed the invitation of the trees
to the river and the sky.
"It is still a beautiful day."

KJB

I used to be afraid of You.
All those fierce words.
I couldn't work You out from the words.

Reverend McInnis used to roar them from the pulpit.
"Damnation". "Gnashing of teeth". "Punishment."…
Afraid of You.

Headmaster Woodhead shouted at assembly when he read them.
And picked his nose at the same time and put his hands in his pockets and pushed his trousers
down so his braces stretched and we laughed quietly at the sight of his shirt tucked in his
underpants, quietly because we were afraid of him.
And afraid of You.

Miss Cowburn had a ruler for our hands and a strap for our bottoms.
Laid out ever so precisely on either side of the Bible on her desk when she read.
I was afraid of her,
And afraid of You.

In R.E. - Reverend Chaplin said, "It means this."
And he got red faced when I said "Not to me."
And I got six of the worst. He said it was Your will, it would cleanse me of sin.
All it cleansed me of was fear of You, and I learned to hate instead.

When I grew up I wandered,
And I read You cover to cover.
None of it was believable.
I didn't like the stories, full of contradictions, like a cheap novel.
Anyway the Beatles made more sense in '67.

What changed? Me or You?
I have spent my days strip mining to get to the nuggets and there You were all along.
I was discovering You, like I discovered my dad long after he was dead.
Gold in the mud, lights in the shadow.

I fell out of fear and into love.
It took me a while,
A while to realise that all along You were letting me know in Your book that You were on my side.
And then when He came (when You came as Him)
That You are with me,
That You are with us.
Then later on, in Pentecostal ecstasy, that You are inside us.
Inside me.
Inside us.

Closer to me than my own breath You are,
Knowing me better than I know myself.

But I never quite got it at first in that book, those books.
Couldn't You have put it in plain language?
A modern idiom?
But then again, I probably wouldn't have believed, we probably wouldn't have believed You.
After all, how to put the silence that speaks through all eternity into words?
All I can do is listen,
To the Words
To the silence in the Words,
To You.
You said, "My Word shall not return to Me void."
What fills the void?
In the silence there is no voice of fear or hatred.
Only love,
When all is read and done, only Love.

Spaces

There have been times when You disappeared
Or at least I thought You did.
Times when I asked, cried out, "Where are You?"
And the question was an echo in the empty
Hangar of my consciousness.
A bit of slurry washed away down Gesthemane's drains.
It was hurtful, this empty space.
I thought You had left me and I was afraid.
And angry; with You and maybe myself.

With myself because it seemed I'd been seduced
By a saccharin possibility of You,
You an invention, a holy coping mechanism
Sweetening the pain of the world.
If You were real, no, loving,
Why did you abandon me? Like the time I got sick
And it looked like I might die.

A space opened up, like the waiting area in an
airport lounge when the 'plane has long gone.
A space like when the tide rolls out and the wet
Pebbles become temporary suns.
A space like a birthroom when the baby is set to come
Into the world but is holding back for hours.
A space like a bedroom when someone is readying to die.
A space where everything is happening but nothing is moving.
A space that feels like punishment or a room full of mistakes.
A space clogged with between-ness, where presence of mind
And absence of mind are held in nervily unstable
Imbalance, whilst anger queues outside the door.
A space where remembering and forgetting
Are held in a hostile, resigned truce.

Looking back I can see the withdrawal wasn't a violation
Nor the reaction to it unpredictable or without reward.
It was pregnant, a *tsim-tsum* where You gave me space
Not as abandonment but as full-filling possibility.
A vacuum not to expel but to draw me deeper into You.
The thought that You were not there, here, was just
A thought to be eventually spiralled away down the
Plughole of untruth, leaving only the truth of these spaces
[Of their potential down the years where forgetting gets
Flipped and remembering fructifies] to no longer be afraid.

Summer storm on Iona

Normally when I hear You speak, every word comes wrapped in silence.
Every syllable drips noiselessly into that space where I think and feel and see.
No tape recorder could ever capture You. You wouldn't show up on an audiograph or some
shimmering monitor lighting up a corner of a studio at Abbey Road.

Today You were as loud as I have ever heard You.
There was nothing private, subtle, about You.
Today all those with eyes to see and ears to hear
Would have known You were here.

The church roof heaved making tensile sounds of minor sexual ecstasy,
Groans that peaked and bowed the beams.
Outside there was more of You being loud in tree and on waves.
You were rattling hotel room doors and the windows of the self-catering.

We were inside, sheltering; said, "because of the rain" or
"the wind will knock you over." But I think it was because we were afraid of You.
You were just too obvious, shaking the island, banging against our eardrums.
When You shout it can't be ignored. Earplugs would be in vain and decapitation extreme.

Best just to listen. If You are making that much noise, best just to listen.
Now, what are You saying? What is it that insists, persists in attention?
Oh, now I hear it, it's Your song isn't it? Being sung in a way that's just
A little bit frightening, a little bit exhilarating.

Singing Your song without us – who's there to listen? That's what You can do,
Compose differently. I'm used to the silent solo, even the quintet, but when You let rip
With the full orchestra, well, then everybody gets to hear You. Even the deaf.
The question is not what made that sound, but Who?

"Answer that!" I heard You say, "And the symphony of time itself will never cease to play for you."
"Play on, please.
Play on."

A field of diamonds

The snow came and the sun woke me, both with silence.
My footprints were those of the first man on the moon.
The sun, busy rising, set fire to Souther Fell.
Had I not looked at that moment, at that precise moment,
I would have missed it. The mire had been replaced.
Replaced by a field of diamonds.

Miss Fletcher shouted not to run, so we did. Out of the
classroom, raincoats flying , wellies clacking. The snow
had come on the last day of school. I had a party hat I'd made -
a white swan with paper wings ("Well done, Stephen").
The sun fell behind the church and we chased flakes of snow.
As the children whirled I saw only a field of diamonds.

My mum condemned the snow and those who ventured out in it.
"Silly fools! Sit by the fire, that's the thing to do. Now where's
those digestives? Let's put the kettle on." Her hands held a biscuit
serenely, hands bruised by floors yet poised more gracefully than the
queen's that time when she drove past our school. The light was on my mum's face as the sun
negotiated the window frame; her hair, a field of diamonds.

My son arrived three months before the December snow.
We put him in his pram in the bay window, so he could watch
it falling, falling from a white sky. So we could watch him
watching the snow falling. His blue in blue birth eyes had turned brown.
It made them deeper somehow.
Deep enough in the half light to reflect a field of diamonds.

When the snow heaves into our valley its always possible the church
will not be open. Prayer might have to confine itself to home and hearth.
Somehow enough people get through. Enough to gather.
If you stand at the front, perhaps by the altar,
perhaps whilst doing a reading – is that just the candlelight dancing
across the bowed heads? Or, here too, a field of diamonds?

Snowstorms in mid-winter. Snowstorms in the long arc of my life.
Each one captured a moment in time, framed it, separated it from
the lost memories. "Do you remember that blizzard of '86, when we got
stuck on a paralysed A66? When we got out of the car afraid? And all our
plans were unravelling? You said, "Not to worry, don't worry love,
look at the view." But I looked at you and saw a field of diamonds.

You came in the snow time, so they say, trailing diamonds in the sky
and have been doing so ever since. The billboard in the street is made of
diamonds made by the diamond light of a neon ribbon. The black slush
is ice-firmed underfoot. In its nature, in its unseen, if we look, if we would
only look, is your face, a Christmas gift, given every day. Wealth
unsurpassable, You, a field of diamonds.

Industrial relations

You may be many things.
I never really know.
But one thing is for sure – You're no wimp.

I mean, the solitary time when we're just sitting there saying "I love you" or when I've arrived with my shopping list, I mean, it comes to an end doesn't it and I hear You say "right, times up, break over, now get out there and work" so sometimes I think it's unfair, I mean to say, no minimum wage, no employment rights, just do as I tell you, I mean what kind of industrial relations is that, and no pension and no possibility of retirement, just work 'till you drop and pray which is the same thing really?

You're a tough employer.
I'm sure there must be some legislation to protect me.
Oh yes, I forgot, the Union rights.

Periphysion

If I place myself
at the centre,
then I am become a God,
blasphemy on two legs
that places You
out there,
somewhere on the periphery.
This is not a place from which You
will administer a rebuke
(although maybe I fear that You will,
an old echo repeats that lie).
I know that You wait there,
loving me.

When eventually,
if I am lucky or
after disciplined work or maybe
after an especially good pudding,
I wake up and see You
at the centre
an odd centre where there is no periphery
except the illusion of one.
Then and only then
I am emptied out.
Then the I who I think I am
waits
to be filled.

Invisible

What I write now is not true.
These words are post-its on a fleeting image.
Too temporary and too thin to describe You.
But there is a kind of darkness filled with so much light that light itself is a shadow.
Flashes of light burst out of You the source of every thing and thought.
Still I am left with this darkness, impenetrable, in which superficial impressions of You rise into significance then fall back into dark incomprehension.
Now and again a little flash pierces the mystery and is gone.
I kid myself I know something.
Shape and form seem to have certainty, meaning.
Then they're gone, never repeated.
Incapable of capture, so tiny, and yet in them a dark star in which all universes are contained.
There is that sense of something, a ghost hovering on the edge of possibility.
As soon as I try to look at it, it's gone, or it changes, or it never was.
Try as I might to refine or define or confine it, it escapes me.
Yet I'm left with something inescapable.
I may not know what it looks like beyond glimpses.
But I'm left with a certainty of knowing what You are.
Love.

The waiting room

The waiting room is full.
I came in some time ago,
although I have no memory of making an appointment.
I've occupied my mind and my self since I passed the entrance.
To pass the time. I've noticed everyone around me is doing the same.
I've noticed others seem to notice, at least some.
Well, the rest seem to be occupied with occupation.

There's a little girl with blue eyes who asks
"Mummy, why have we come here?"
Mummy seems unwilling or unable to answer.
Or perhaps the chocolate she offers is her reply.
I'm not sure when my appointment will be called.
You keep Your diary secret.
I guess I just have to wait my turn.
Like everyone else.

The library

I've read a lot of books about You.
Some of them indifferent.
Some of them inspiring.
The best ones all seemed to have the same author
'though the names were unto themselves.
Nevertheless they all seemed to say, after a while,
the same things,
in different ways,
but the same things.
So it made me wonder
if there was a lot of plagiarism about.
Truth comes dressed for dancing.
She wears a different costume governed
by the fashion of the day
but she's still the same truth underneath.
I asked myself why I kept reading
seeing as everything after a while tasted undifferentiated.
Somewhere out of sight a bird sang, "But you just want to know."
Another, perhaps a night owl, wheezed, "And to know that you already know."
That's why real knowing is only remembering.
I could have kept adding books to the shelves.
Mike said, "You've got more books than I've had hot dinners."
A fast seemed a good idea.
Then in a quiet moment You offered a final volume.
Quite big.
But only one sentence.
"If you want more, become your own book; yourself the reading."

Whitsuntide 1956

Somebody said "Australia", in the way of conversation.
I saw everyone's lips moving, but the sound had been switched off.
Another memory crept in, from long ago…

Australia was a long way off. I knew this because
Miss Cowburn said so. And my dad.
And my mum, who said "You could get there
for ten pounds. And it was always sunny."
Well, I know when my mum took me shopping
in Bury it cost three pence on the bus
and it seemed to take ages to get there.
And I knew that there were, oh, loads of
three pences in ten pounds so Australia must
have been miles away.
At least further than Bury.

I could see them all coming up the hill.
The scholars. I knew they were scholars because
Grandma Walmsley said
"Isn't it lovely to see the scholars?" But I wasn't sure
if the scholars were the dresses on the girls or the men
in the brass bands, or maybe the banners.

I asked my mum why they were marching.
And she said, "Because they like to." And "For God".
I said "Where's God?" (looking down the long line of
scholars, way down the hill, and round the bend
where I could not see. They kept coming.)
She said "A long way off."
And I said "Bury?"
And she said "No, much further."
And I said "Australia?"
And she said "Sort of."

And they kept coming up the hill. Up Ainsworth Road.
Kept coming. And when we went home, they were still coming.
So I never got to see God,
who I thought must be bringing up the rear.
Like my dad did sometimes.
When he had his "specials" uniform on.
I liked my dad in his uniform. I was so proud of him.
I used to run after my friends Eric and Alan
to get them to come and look at him. He was my dad.
When he had his uniform on he was bigger.

God had to be at the end of the parade.
I supposed he'd have to be at the end.
Coming all the way from Australia.

...Across the tremendous bridge of time
I send You this gift of remembrance,
a child's eye view, or perhaps a letter I wrote
and forgot to post then rediscovered at the
back of a drawer.
But now, oh now, how very, very close You are.

The Nightmare of Gerontius

Who took all the time away?
Did I accidentally press the "delete" button?
Or did all the years get shredded in the machine by the office chair?
Have they been recycled, or just so much landfill?

I sit on the bench on the cliff-top watching the sea.
I'm content to watch.
No ambition for exercise or possession of any particular movement.
I have the feeling that the sea is watching me.

When I was a kid I watched the old people on the promenade with
their fish and chips.
Sitting on the benches.
Watching.
They had grey hair.

I've had my fish and chips.
And I'm sitting on a bench on the promenade.
Watching.
I have grey hair.

I've been mugged of time by time.
She crept up on me by the stairwell when I wasn't looking, when
I was busy planning something or watching TV or waiting for the
night to come.
She crept up and she stole the lot.

And now I sit.
Condensed.
Watching the sea.
I have become my own thin volume, a little book.

Stacked library shelves stretch beyond the timeless horizon.
New books are being added all the time.
So many.
Room for one more.

Red Admiral

I don't know who it was first shouted "A red admiral!"
I'm not sure it was one of us.
Maybe Mrs. Morris standing by the gate in her pinnie.
That would have been unusual.
She hated kids.

But we all took up the cry and maybe, oh, a dozen
ran after it up the road. It was ahead of us,
fluttering, and above us, but we ran after it. I still
don't know why. Running after things for no reason
is what kids do.

Running up Red Bank Road, flanked by houses in red brick.
It had blood red flashes on its wings.
We went red faced with running 'till it disappeared.
I guess they've been my favourites ever since:
red admirals.

Once in late autumn some stayed alive under the cool sun.
The little house beneath Helvellyn had grand views.
A delayed sedum in the garden fed them. And so did I.
I put honey on my fingers and they would land to feed.
Quite fearless.

They're here now in this valley, where foxes mock the hounds.
Have they followed me from all those years ago?
If they have a message, it's hidden from me.
Someone said butterflies will lick the salt from a corpse.
Not yet, Beloved, not yet.

Lent

Sometimes a kind of claustrophobia sets in.
Events conspire; cold, wet events.
Forgetting rises up like a winter fog.
And then I remember, perhaps by prayer
Or a moment when the chocolate tastes especially good
Or the soft touch of skin on skin.
And then I remember…You.

Sometimes a kind of boundlessness sets in.
Possibility expands; breezy, rising possibility.
Hope rises up like spring buds.
And then I remember, perhaps by song
Or a moment when the wine bursts on my tongue
Or the sound of a grandchild sleeping.
And then I remember…You.

Sometimes a kind of glory sets in.
Stillness rises; warm, sultry stillness.
The not-much-happening of a hot summer evening.
And then I remember, perhaps by pilgrimage
Or a moment when a bee collides with my cheek
Or a young buzzard rises for the first time.
And then I remember…You.

Sometimes a kind of hollowness sets in.
Decay grips; falling, colour-changing decay.
The shrivelling up and collapsing of things of an autumn reclamation.
And then I remember, perhaps by contradiction,
Or a sudden chill of the heat by disappointment or impending death
Or a blackberry haloed by dewdrops.
And then I remember…You.

All my seasons are in You.
You are all my seasons.
Difference is merely a thought.
All of them.
All of You.
Here.
Now.
Always.

Part 2

You to me

Jump

Are you waiting for Me?
The queue is a long one.
Jump!
See? It was unnecessary, lining up.
I don't make conditions.
You might think I do,
But that's just a thought.
Come when you're ready.
No pressure.
No requirements.
Jump the queue
And you'll find there wasn't one really.
Only in your imagination.
I'm right here.
Where are you looking?
Over there?
I'm right here.
Here!

Dancing

When you fell in love with Me,
wasn't that when I asked you to dance?
It doesn't matter what everyone else is doing,
from cosmic jitterbug to serene glide.
It doesn't matter.
A loving relationship like ours makes its own steps.
Tentatively, at first, I reassured you.
Reassured you that I wouldn't step on your toes.
Slowly you came to see that a relationship like ours
is a waltz across the dance floor of time.
Just the two of us spinning and spinning.
Anyone watching from the outside would swear
they saw two set off.
Swear to it.
And swear to it now that both had blurred into one.
Still dancing.

Lonesome pine

If you look hard enough
You'll always find an island.
Water has nothing to do with it.
Look at that line in the airport, that man there,
With the blue shoulder bag.
Just look at his eyes.
See?
He's completely alone.

And that girl, in the purple dress,
Stroking her long blond hair
Whilst everyone around her is ordering their food.
Look at her eyes.
See?
She could be sitting under a solitary palm
On an isolated atoll
Somewhere in the tropics.

Along the footpath, people coming and going,
But look what happens when you step off and sit
Under the pine tree.
The one bordered by shingle and bitter, broken gorse.
Try it. Sit there.
See?
It could just as well be a planet alone,
Without populace.

If you want time with Me on an island,
You'll find Me on an island if you look.
Nearer than you think.
There, right under your nose.
Everything you ever need to know,
The solitude you seek,
Right inside you. Right there.
See?

Confession

I heard your whispered, "I need You."
I'm glad you've admitted it.
Nothing wrong with needing.
Needing is recognising something you can't do without.
Something your very life depends upon.
Desire distracts, delays, destroys.
But need, now you've admitted it, is the lifeblood between us.
Humility is not the acquisition of self, of the power of now,
Of the power of self containment…
But the surrender of them; sacrament.
Humbled into powerlessness, you know you need Me.
Now look how close we have become.

Commandment

Honour thy father and thy mother.
Pay tribute to that which birthed you.
Just because you were fed by these wombs
And then escaped them, does not mean that you did not need them once.
Remember.
Remember.

You've been held and nurtured, safely, along the Way.
These places.
These people.
These ways of worship.
Remember.

Sometimes the foods were sweet.
Sometimes bitter.
But they made you.
The man.

My servants get to taste all the ingredients before they cook a really fine dish.
Such recipes!
Such flavours!
I have spiced and salted and sweetened your life from the beginning.
Now see what menu you can come up with.
Cook!

Findhorn Bay

The yellow sea,
Bordering the hinterland in May.
There is a desert where the gorse edges into the dunes.
Taking the hint you climbed the one crowned
With thorns.

I like to surprise you.
There, where the gorse could find no purchase;
A colony of violets.
These impossible flowers among inhospitable gravel.
Get the picture?

Even in the desert, you can still bloom.
Don't worry about the dry bones in the desiccated lands of My religion.
I'll water you.
Put down your roots.
And bloom.

Savouring

You'll remember that meal at Reveillon?
How it lasted?
Lasted all night long?

That's the way to eat.
Slowly.
Savouring each taste. Sharing the experience.

Treat My words the same way.
Digest them.
Slowly.

Meaning is like a symphony.
Rush it through and you'll miss the detail.
All the little notes will escape you.

Savour Me.

And while you're taking that in (slowly)
consider this. When words are born they always need a
slow birth.

Slow food is best
and so are
slow words.

Prayer in heaven

Do they pray in heaven?

I'll answer that for you;
of course not.

That's not because there isn't a heaven
or because they've all given up on praying.

You see there's no need to pray a prayer, no need at all,
when you have become one.

Meanwhile, why wait until then?

Make your life a prayer.

Now.

Promise

You'll remember My promise to you,
"I am with you always."
You can find Me in dance and dream if you want to.
But really, I'm with you,
Always.
Even to the end of time.
And in that moment when you know Me,
That moment that keeps lasting longer and longer,
Then in that moment, time has ended, and
I am, with you.

Gorbalsiona

We can meet and greet anywhere.
You think it's easier on the island;
This rare place?

Why should it be anywhere any different?
Think about it.
Take a peep under the dustbin lid on the corner of Eglinton Street.

Or lift your gaze up the concrete walls of Stirlingfaulds.
Way up, to the twenty fifth floor.
And while you're looking, notice how you can't not notice the background din.

The materials and the lights and the colours and the sound and the smells
Are all the same as Iona.
Just arranged differently.

Now ask Who arranged them.
Now answer the question.
Then maybe you'll see we can meet and greet anywhere.

Invitation

It wasn't won without hard work.
Remember, I sweat blood.
It was a price worth paying to let you drink it.
Drink it since those first days by the altar,
leaning on the bar, kneeling on the soft, blood-red carpet.
Wine intoxicates.
Get drunk with Me.
I invited you to the bar, you accepted.
Now dance with Me, and sweat.
Do it now while the fire of life rages about you.
The dead, being bloodless, do not sweat.
Is that what you want?
We both know the answer.
So dance with Me, put the cross on your back.
No matter how heavy it gets, see, you can still
trip the light fantastic.
Soon we'll pirouette out of the world together.
They'll clap us out of the ballroom.
Who wouldn't at the sight of a pas-de-deux like that?

Rose

How many times will you sit here?
Waiting?
There's a rose growing in the garden
behind you.
Turn around, her petals are touching
your shoulder.
The smell of roses, coming from
behind you.
The shadows on the screen in front of you are their own seduction.
They cannot touch you on the shoulder
or fill your head with the scent of Love.
Turn around.

Dry land

Over there, the dry land.
Your feet are on firm ground.
Flat earth, beaten by many feet.

Standing up, you have a good view.
You can see Me from there.
I am on the poolside bench.

Over there, you can be sure
you will not get splashed.
Come, sit on My bench.

Better still,
come on in,
the water's lovely.

Eternity

Why on earth do you wonder what happens next?
Look at that bee, hoovering the flowers.
She has no thought of past or future.
Or present, come to that.
She's not worried about eternity.
She's living it.
Now.

At the centre of the cross,
where time and space intersect,
He was suspended.
And escaped them both.
You can do the same.
No need to hang yourself dutifully
on one of Borrowdale's yews.

The question was multiple choice.
Only one answer.
Watch that bee, and that flower.
Or the whole of creation if you care to.
Do you notice a difference?
Of course not.
How much more obvious can I make it?

The Gaze

It took you a while to realise I was gazing at you.
On reflection, you can see the precise time when you would pay attention was in the contract.

(There is some small print, but I shouldn't worry about that
for the time being.)

Everyone's wake-up call is set.
It's interesting to speculate who set it.

When you woke up, do you remember?
Do you remember that you gazed back at Me?

My eyes met yours and it was Love at first sight.
There may be two of us, but there's only one gaze.

Direction

There's a lot of room for manoeuvre in this opulent landscape.
Why don't you pick up your map and visit some of the sites?

Better still, you could try exploring the blank spaces;
Discovering landmarks for yourself, maybe even create some of your own.

Don't worry; I'll help you find your way back.
I haven't lost anybody yet.

Since you asked

I am like this lighthouse,
earth and sky bound,
splicing shadows,
protesting the gale,
immovable,
but I will last longer.

I am like this sea,
swelling and deep,
covering secrets,
boiling with life,
unfathomable,
but I will last longer.

I am like this harbour,
full and welcoming,
gathering ships,
mingling peoples,
insatiable,
but I will last longer.

I am like this dolphin,
sleek and masterly,
piercing the waters,
seeing two worlds,
indomitable,
but I will last longer.

I am like this day,
shimmering and rainless,
stretching sky to sky,
grounding time,
ungovernable,
but I will last longer.

I am like this night,
star splattered,
moon sliding,
converging shadows,
uncompromising,
but I will last longer.

I am like time,
holding to account,
fulfilling promises,
fructifying possibilities,
impenetrable,
but I will last longer.

I am like you.

The claxon

The claxon sounds "original sin!"
Tablets of stone make stone hearts.
My rule is quite simple.
Don't listen to it.
A lie is still a lie no matter how strong the liar.
My song beats in your heart.
Listen to it.
You know there is a harmony there.
So do I.
After all, I put it there;
The sound of your original blessing.
Who will you believe, the claxon or Me?

Cairns

From a distance the fells are deceptive.
They look like velvet, soft to touch.
Up close, Carrock has wild sides,
hidden water holes and boulders set wide
like gin traps hungry for an unwary ankle.
You could get lost, even die here.
You could stay safe in your car.
Admire the view.

Julie said, "Up there? No thanks!"
How wrong she was. The hills are
full of gratitude. Take a closer look
at the deceptive wild. The cairns
carry report of the ones who set off
before you. They do not know
deception. Follow the markers
but be sure that you will fall,
in Love.

Great expectation

As there is nothing new under the sun,
you could try the moonlight.
You'll find Me there too, wearing My night attire.
Prepare to be seduced.
When dawn comes you will find I have made everything new.
Especially for you.

Crows

Don't be alarmed by the circling of the carrion crows while you lie there.
Just tell them you're not dead yet.
Death and repose look the same to them, but only the dead hold their interest.
No need to make a big show of it, save energy for the movement that matters.
Try flicking your little finger now and then, it will suffice, it's all the warning they need.
Meanwhile just keep dying into life; the crows will find lunch elsewhere.

Promise

The lurch into darkness is frightening.
I know, I've been there too.
I am there now, even though you can't see me.
I didn't send you there, here.
That's an old lie from long ago.
Look deep, even the darkness is illumined.
We had an agreement; it hasn't expired yet.
You signed up for it, willingly if you look.
Don't be distracted by Manichean stories;
stories of duality to frighten the children.
Remember it's all One and there will be
a time and a place, where there is no time
and no place that you will remember.
Remember the agreement.
I never made any promises about not
suffering or not being sad or that there
would be no darkness. But I did promise
that I would never to leave you. And I
did promise that you will come Home.

On the stage

We have an agreement.
You went where you are, willingly, remember?
You were watching the drama and asked "Can I try that?"
I said "Yes, but there's no rewriting the role, you have to take what comes.
There's only one name on the Director's chair, and it's Mine."
Remember?
And you said "No problem, bring it on, I'll try anything."
So when it gets tough, don't turn to Me and complain.

We have an agreement.
In your heart of hearts, you wouldn't want to change it would you?
It's a juicy part; the performance of a lifetime.
And you'll get far more than an Oscar.

The salesman

You'll have noticed by now how everybody is selling something.
Noticed especially in the big city;
everybody hustling and hassling.

I've got the best produce on the market.
Notice how I don't make a song and dance about it.
That's because a song and a dance are what I'm selling.

Well, not selling exactly, more like giving away.
And big discounts too. Discounts and cost free?
How cool is that!

Come on, try My stall, there's never any queue and
I give cast iron guarantees.
The city is noisy, but check My sales pitch.

You'll hear Me calling day and night.
"Love for sale."
Are you buying?

Terminal

So, things are going wrong.
That ticker isn't ticking like it used to.
And I hear the endocrinologist zapped your thyroid.
The back pain I know about too.
You've complained about it long enough.
And now Mr Barrett's namesakes have moved in,
Revelling in a champagne lubricated sanctuary.

I see the other end's had a visitor too.
That little chestnut's proliferation has been fingered.
Oh, and your eyes have kept the optician wealthy.
Your ears are now untroubled by half the noise around you.
I heard the audiologist, a young slip of a thing, tell you.
"It's called getting old."
Tell Me about it!

I haven't forgotten you.
Don't make this an excuse to run away.
You've tried that before.
It didn't work then.
It won't work now.
Some say life is an incurable disease.
They're wrong.

There's One relief.
I've got the patent on it.
I issued the license long ago by a dead sea.
No prescription charges of course.
Cheaper than the NHS really.
Everybody gets the treatment in the end.
There's no getting away from Me.

You said to Me, "It's OK for You.
You don't know what it's like.
Disease and death and the fear of both."
You're wrong.
Remember My story.
Remember Golgotha and the run-up to it.
So don't tell Me I don't know.

Remember I won.
And so will you.
Even if you don't believe Me, when I say you're not alone.
I'm there, here, in spite of you.
The story books have angels with white fluffy wings.
Yours come with white coats bearing needles and pharmacology.
It doesn't mean they're not heaven sent.

They're still angels, even in sterile gowns and gloves.
Watch and wait.
Watch and wait.
The script is being written as we speak.
Like all good storytellers I keep the end a surprise.
Except, of course, you know the end.
It's only a beginning.

The missed boat

Will you not love Me?
Will you not love Me when the last leaves have fallen?
Oh, there is no time left.
The waterbutt is empty.
The wine drunk.
Only fools hang by the harbour wall.
The last of the ferries has departed.
Those without tickets stare at the empty sea.
Their hopes shrivel over the weedless crevices.
Time passes.
Clinging is impossible.
Will you not love Me?
Listen, I have a plan.
Take My ticket.
There's plenty of yachts in the next bay.
See, I always come up trumps.
How's that for mastery?
I told you I was in charge.
Not bad eh?
Don't worry.
I've got the full passenger list.
I have a helper who ticks them off, one by one.
We're a good team.
The system works.
We've been at it long enough.
Do you really need to see My qualifications?
Of course not.
Now do you see you still love Me?

Faith

If you are asking for proof,
you could try a double blind randomised controlled trial.
Listen.
Isn't your heart speaking the truth?
Has she ever told you a lie?
Surrender proof.
That's faith.

Silence

When the hills fall silent no passing aircraft ripple the stillness.
The deep of Bassenthwaite has muffled the sound of straggling cars.
The still air does not even whisper between the pines and your ears.
If you sit in this silence you can listen to waiting.

The soundless world is deafening compared to My silence.

Auto da Fe

If you really want to hear Me I mean really want to hear
Me then somewhere along the line you're going to have
to switch off all the noise you use to drown Me out
whether it's the noise on the outside or the noise on the
inside both of which intentionally or otherwise serve
to make sure you can avoid hearing Me and deafen you
to My still small voice that will never go away no matter
how long you keep it up and fool yourself at least for
a while that you can avoid listening to Me and when
you do and it's a question of when not if whether you
believe Me or not because I'm never going to give up
on you so when you finally get that then maybe you will
finally surrender and hear My...........................

Silence

About the author

Reverend Professor Stephen G. Wright FRCN MBE

Stephen works as a spiritual director for the Sacred Space Foundation (see www.sacredspace.org.uk) helping those in spiritual crisis and guiding spiritual seekers. Before this he had a long and distinguished history in academia and in the British National Health Service, as a council member of the Royal College of Nursing, secondment to the Department of Health and a consultant to the W.H.O. He has worked in over 60 different countries advising on nursing and health care development and written many nursing books and scholarly papers. He is an editorial adviser to Nursing Standard with regular columns on the politics and spirituality of nursing and health and an Honorary Fellow of the University of Cumbria where he is developing a spiritually based leadership programme. He took a decided turn out of mainstream nursing (or was taken!) following an intense period of spiritual awakening and since than has co-authored two books exploring the nature of healing relationships - "Therapeutic Touch" and "Sacred Space – right relationship and spirituality in health care" (both co-written with Jean Sayre-Adams). "Reflections on spirituality and health" published in 2005, by Wiley, received outstanding reviews. "Coming Home" was published in 2009, a personal and scholarly account of spiritual awakening rooted in the experience of his work as a spiritual director, for which he received significant training in the presence of several renowned teachers and at the Interfaith Seminary (www.theinterfaithfoundation.com). He is an active trustee of several charities and a Member of the Iona Community. He works with organisations developing the practice of healing, spiritual care, conflict resolution and staff support. He is an ordained interfaith minister and spiritual director and brings a rich experience of spiritual practice from many faiths to his work. His spiritual exploration, described in "Coming Home" led to his return to Christianity, following the contemplative way and the loving and inclusive path mapped out by the Iona Community. His published work includes songs, chants, dances ("Song and dance for the Way Home" 2010) and poetry ("Beloved" 2011) and other works ("Burnout" 2010, "Contemplation" 2011). He lives in the English Lake District, deepening service and spiritual practice, participating in his local church community, taking care of his organic garden and enjoying grandfatherhood.

www.ingramcontent.com/pod-product-compliance
Lightning Source LLC
Chambersburg PA
CBHW060146050426
42448CB00010B/2320